MY FIRST STEP

ATTAIN THE OBJECTIVE

ARUNDHATI KAR

Made with ♥ on the Notion Press Platform
www.notionpress.com

Deadicated to my grandfather(ex Army officer),who help me to take my first step,also shows me the right path to broad my vision range.

Contents

Foreword

I am Arundhati kar,from Bhadrak. This is my first book,where i try to write poetry,motivational quotes and my thoughts.I hope this book will help you to take your first step.Happy reading

Preface

My hobbies are writing poem,short story,so i first started writing small quotes. This is my first book,through this book i want to spread my thoughts and motivate our generation.

1. NAYA SAAL

Khushiyan jinme dale dhere
jitne tere utne mere
naye saal ki packet me hai
365 naye sabere
din me 100 100 bar dikhenge
chahat ka akbar likhenge
eak dujhe ka hat pakd ke
her panhe pe pyar likhenge
rahengi khushiyan harper gehre
365 naye sabere

2. BE YOUR OWN SANTA

Dushronki khushi me sath dena konsi badibat hai
kabhi unke dukh me sath deke to dekho
Dushronki dhuk ki wajah banke kya fayada hai
kabhi unki khushi ki wajah to banke dekho
Dushronse umeed lagake kya fayada hai
kabhi khud pe umeed lagake to dekho
Dushron ko santa banake apni wish pura karne se kya maja hai
kabhi khudka santa khud banke to dekho

3. MODERN WORLD-SHOULD FOLLOW

Ajj kalke jamaneme ego,attitude,misunderstanding ke bich pyar kahin dab sa gaya hai.

jise dekho matlab or paisa ki piche bhagta rehta hai.

kya ea jamana aur iss jamane ke log pehle jaisa nahi ho sakte,

janha pyar important ho ego nahi.

janha rishte important ho paisa nahi.

janha pyar me kabhi interest kam na ho.

janha rishte matlab se nahi dill se nibhaya jata ho.

janha batein timepass ke liye nahi eak dushreko samjh ne ke liye kiya ja raha ho.

4. REEL LIFE

Yanha sab manzil ki talash me hain
koi suffer ki baat kyun nahi karta?
jise dekho bas bhag hi raha hai
koi doopal bethkar pyar se baat kyun nahi karta?

5. KHUBSHHURTI

Khubshurti jo dill se dekh sake
wo hai khubshurti
jise na dhup ki fhikar ho na kabhi chao ki
wo hai khubshurti
ankho ki gehrai hai khubshurti
insan ki surat nahi sirat hai khubshurti

6. STORY OF FEELINGS

Once there was an ISLAND where all the feelings lived together.one day,there came a storm in the sea and the island was about to drawn.Every feelings was scared but love made a boat escape.All the feelings jumped in the boat except for one feelings.Love got down to see what it was...it was EGO(Son of misunderstanding).Love tried and tried but ego didn't move.Everyone told love to leave ego and come in the boat but love was meant to love.It remained with ego!all other feelings were left alive but love died because of EGO.........!

7. KHUDKO BEHTAR BANAO

Dushronki madat karnese pehle,

khudki madat karna cahiye.

Dushronki galtiyan nikalnese pehle,

khudki galtiyan sudhar na cahiye.

Dushron se pyar karne se pehle,

khudse pyar karna ana cahiye.

Dushron ko samjh ne ke liye,

pehle khudko samjho.

8. TIPS

1.Future is nothing but an outcome of our decision,
make the right decision and your future will be right.
2.EK din apne aap se isstarha miloge ki zindegi khubshurat
lagne lagegi.
3.Imaginary life se bahar nikal kar,real life me aao
kyunki aage jakar iss ke sath hi pala padna hai.
4.Whatever you are doing ,do with a good intention.
5.Be there for others but never leaves behind yourself.
6.Don't lose the spark that makes you...you.
7.TRUST is inversely proportional to communication.

The End

NEVER STOP DREAMING

KHUSHI SINHA

*THIS STORY DEDICATED TO THE LIFE
OF THE DREAM . HOW OUR LIFE
PROCESS STARTING TO END WITH
DREAMS HOW WE SEE DREAMS AND
HOW IT COMPLTE .*

Contents

Foreword

DEAR READERS ,

WHO IS READING BOOK RIGHT NOW,

THIS STORY IS VERY SIMPLE TO READ.FOR UNDERSTANDING THE MAIN MOTIVATE FEEL AND READ THEN YOU CAN UNDERSTAND THE MAIN MEANING OF THE STORY.

Preface

THIS IS THE STORY A DREAMY GIRL. SHE DREAMS ALOT. SHE LIVED WITH HER PARENTS IN DELHI. HAR PARENTS ARE TEACHERS SHE STRUGGLE IN HER . SHE LOSTS, SAD, FACE WITH DISEASE AND HAT. SHE CAN'T ENJOY HER CHILDEN VERSION .

NEVER STOP DREAMING

KRITIKA

THIS IS THE STORY OF DELHI SINCE 2001 . ON 6/2/ 2001 BORNS A CUTE GIRL IN HINDU FAMILY NAMED KRITIKA . HER PARENTS ARE TEACHERS .7 YEARS AGO. SINCE 2008 . NOW SHE IS 7 YEAR OLD.NOW THIS THE STORY OF A GIRL DREAMY LIFE . SHE DREAMS ALOT . SHE IS FULL HAPPINESS, CUTENESS, LOVEABLE , HONEST , INTELLIGENT ,CARING AND FUNNY GIRL..SHE IS IN CLASS 1ST . SHE MEET VEER HE IS A BOY . VEER'S FATHER IS A DOCTOR. KRITIKA AND VEER ARE BEST FRIEND . KIRITKA TAKES HIS SISTER'S NUMBER TO TALK WITH HIM ON CALLS .

VEER AND KRITIKA TALKING

SHE CHANGES THE SCHOOL AFTER FINAL EXAMS SHE SAID HER DAD WHY I CHANGE THE SCHOOL.PARENTS SAID THIS SCHOOL IS NOT GOOD FOR YOUR EDUCATION.SHE IS

TALKING WITH HER DAD

JUST 7 YEARS OLD SHE CAN,T UNDERSTAND WHY THIS SCHOOL IS NOT FOR MY EDUCATION.SHE THINKS I HAVING THE VEER SISTER'S NUMBER I CAN TALK WITH HIM ON CALLS. SHE CHANGES THE SCHOOL . SOME DAYS AGO THE PHONE SUDDENLY OFFED AND VEER SISTER'S NUMBER IN THAT PHONE IS NOW OFFED SHE WAS IN TENSION SHE THINKS NOW I NEVER TALK WITH HIM .HER MOTHER BUY A NEW PHONE AND ADD SIM CARD FROM OLD PHONE

KIRITKA THINKS MAYBE I CAN TALK WITH VEER SHE SEARCH NUMBER ON NEW PHONE WITH OLD SIM BUT HER NUMBER IS NOT SHOWING NOW SHE WAS SAD HER MOTHER DON'T BE SAID MAKE A NEW BEST FRIEND SHE WAS SAID OK BUT INNER SHE WAS SAD... 3 YEARS AGO..SHE NOW 10 YEARS OLD SHE IS TRYING TO MAKE NEW FRIENDS BUT ALL SAYS I DON'T WANT BE YOUR FRIEND. SHE CAN'T UNDERSTAND WHY KNOW BE HER FRIEND.MAYBE THE ISSUE IS THAT SHE SAY WHAT'S ON HER MIND .ALL ONE STARTING SAYING YOU ARE RUDE I HATE YOU.IN THE SMALL AGE SHE FACES THIS....NOW SHE DECIDED NOW I NEVER MAKE FRIENDS NEVER EVER......NOW SHE IS REALLY BE RUDE...NOW HER DREAMS CAME IN HER LIFE.SHE LOVES CUTE KAWAII STATIONERIES , BAGS, SHOPPING, TRAVELLING ,FAMS, AND HER BIG DREAM HER OWN DESIGN INTIOR HOUSE AND SHE WANTS TO BECOME IPS. SHE LIVED WITH PARENTS IN SMALL HOUSE . NOW SHE WANT BIG HOUSE AND CAR....NOW HER DREAMS IS HER LIFE....EVERY YEAR SHE THINKS NOW I CAN ACHIEVE DREAMS BUT SHE CAN'T HER PARENTS COMPLETING HER EXPENSES..BUT THEY CAN'T BE COMES HER BIG DREAMS THEY VERY MUCH TRYING TO COMING HER DREAMS .2 YEARS AGO . SHE THINKS SHOULD I ALSO START EARNIG TO COMPLETING MY DREAMS AND PARENTS HELP.SHE SMALL GIRL BUT THINKS ALOT . SHE IS TRYING TO EARN ONLINE BUT SHE CAN'T ABLE TO EARN..SHE THINKS CAN I STOP DREAMING NO NO DREAM IS MY LIFE I CAN'T STOP DREAMING ....HER PARENTS SAYS DON'T IMAGINE YOUR DREAMS IT WELL NOT COMPLETE. HER PARENTS TRYING TO UNDERSTANDING HER THAT KEEP PATIENCES..YOUR

DREAM WELL COMPLETE SOON..1 YEAR AGO . SINCE 2014 06/2/2014 ON HER BIRTHDAY HER PARENTS DO OUTING WITH KRITIKA TO MAKE HER HAPPY . THEN IN EVENING HER PARENTS DECIDED TO SUPRISE HER WITH DECORTION,CAKE AND GIFTS THEY PLAN CUTE SUPRISE FOR HER FIRST TEENAGER BIRTHDAY.

CUTE SUPRISE FOR HER

THEN SAW THE DECORTION , CAKE AND GIFT AND SHE WAS VERY HAPPY . BEFORE BLOWING SHE

WISHES THAT MY ALL THE DREAMS COME TRUE AND I MEET FRIEND VEER ALSO. THEN SHE BLOW THE CANDLE AND CUT THE CAKE.NOW SHE WAS 13 YEAR OLD AND THEN HER PARENTS GIFTS HER A CUTE RABBIT SOFT TOY AND HER PARENTS SAYS THIS YOUR BEST FRIEND THATS NEVER HATES YOU SHE SMILE AND SAYS TO SOFT TOY YOUR NAME IS BUNNY YOUR MY BEST FRIEND . THAT CAN NEVER END .HER HAPPIEST DAY EVER IN HER LIFE.

KRITIKA WITH HER BUNNY HER BIRTHDAY VIBES

NEXT WEEK SHE IS NOT FEELING WELL SHE FEELS LIKE HEADACHES,BLURRED VISION,LOSS OF

BLANACE,CONFUSION AND SEIZURES. HER PARENTS ARE VERY CONFUSED WHAT THEY DO. THEY SUDDENLY WENT TO DOCTOR . HER CHECKUP STARTED. DOCTOR SAID SHE HAD BRAIN CANCER IN LAST STAGE WE HAVE TO ADMIT HER FASTER THAN FASTER . BY THE WAY WE CAN'T SAVE HER . AFTER HEARING THIS SHE SHOCKED MY DREAMS CAN'T COMPLTE . SHE STOPPED DREAMING . SHE SAID MY DREAMS NEVER COMPLTE. I WILL DIE NO MY PARENTS MY

CRYING AND SHOCKED KRITIKA

DREAMS.SHE FEELS THIS IS BECAUSE OF MY DREAMS . I NEVER DREAM AGAIN. SHE STARTED CRYING. HER PARENTS SAID DON'T CRY WE WILL

SAVE YOU. HER PARENTS SAID PLEASE START TREATMENT FAST . DOCTOR SAID OK DEPOSIT 2LAKH RUPEES FOR HER TREATMENT ON COUNTER . HER PARENTS SAID TO DOCTOR WE WILL PAY AFTER TREATMENT . NO FIRST DEPOSIT 2 LAKH RUPEES THAN WE CAN START TREATMENT . THEY SAID WE TRY TO COLLECT MONEY FASTER .THEY ARE CONFUSED WHAT WE DO 2 DAYS AFTER HER CONDITION BECAME CRITICAL. THEY DECIDED TO BREAK THEIR FIXED DEPOSIT { FD }. THEY DEPOSIT THE MONEY. HER TREATMENT STARTED. SHE FEELS I CAN'T ALIVE NOW. SHE DEPRESSED SO HER CONDTION BECAME MORE CRITICAL. ONE DAY DOCTOR CAME WITH HIS SON VEER . YES THAT VEER KRITIKA'S FRIEND . VEER SHOCKED TO SEE HER ON BED . SHE IS VERY HAPPY TO SEE HIM . BOTH ARE CRYING . SHE SAID I WILL DIE . NO NO MY FATHER IS THE BEST DOCTOR HE SAVE YOU . SHE ALSO TAIK ABOUT HER DREAM . I WILL STOP DREAMING I AM HERE BECAUSE OF MY DREAM.DON'T WORRY . YOUR DREAM COMPLTE SOON . IF DREAM IS YOUR LIFE SO, NEVER STOP DREAMING YOU CAN ACHIEVE YOUR DREAMS. HE IS TRYING TO MOTIVATE HER. SHE ALSO SAYS I CAN ACHIEVE MY DREAM, I CAN ACHIEVE MY DREAM.VEER ALSO SAYS . YOU CAN ACHIEVE YOUR DREAMS .YOU CAN ACHIEVE YOUR DREAM.SOME DAYS AFTER SHE FIGHT WITH HER CANCER RECOVERS AND GOING BACK TO HOME AND SHE THANKS TO VEER AND HIS FATHER VEER SAID DON'T THANKS TO ME THANKS TO YOUR DREAMS . YOUR DREAM GIVE A MOTIVATION TO ALIVE. SHE SMILES AND HUG HIM TIGHTLY. WE WILL MET SOON.AFTER SOME YEARS IN 2019 . HER PARENTS PROMOTED IN

SCHOOL FOR PRINICIPAL AND VICE PRINICIPAL .

KRITIKA IN AGE OF 18

KRITIKA STUDIES ALOT SHE GOES LONDON FOR HER STUDIES . SHE ACHIEVE HER DREAM.SHE BECOME THE BEST AN ONCOLOGIST.SHE BUY A LUXURY HOUSE AND CAR. THE RICH GIRL OF DELHI . AND WEDS WITH HIS BEST FRIEND VEER IS ALSO AN ONCOLOGIST.SO ,THIS THE STORY OF A DREAMY GIRL . SHE DREAMS ALOT.

MORAL : TRY TRY BUT DON'T CRY JUST KEEP PATIENCE BUT NEVER DREAMING.